Th
at the Seaside

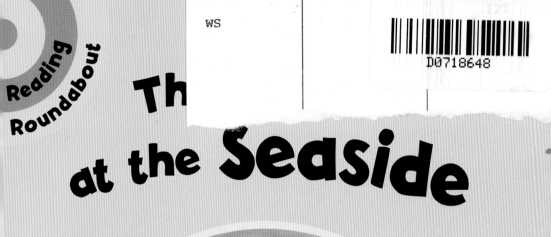

Paul Humphrey

Photography by C

W
FRANKLIN WATTS
LONDON • SYDNEY

First published in 2006 by
Franklin Watts
338 Euston Road
London NW1 3BH

Franklin Watts Australia
Hachette Children's Books
Level 17/207 Kent Street
Sydney NSW 2000

WORCESTERSHIRE COUNTY COUNCIL	
701	
Bertrams	15.04.07
J577.69	£3.99
WS	

© 2006 Franklin Watts

ISBN: 0 7496 6605 6 (hbk)
ISBN: 0 7496 6855 5 (pbk)

Dewey classification number: 394.26942

A CIP catalogue record for this book is available
from the British Library.

Planning and production by Discovery Books Limited
Editor: Rachel Tisdale
Designer: Ian Winton
Photography: Chris Fairclough
Series advisors: Diana Bentley MA and Dee Reid MA,
Fellows of Oxford Brookes University

The author, packager and publisher would like to thank
the following people for their participation in this book:
Auriel Austin-Baker; Arrandeep Bola and family; Lucas Tisdale.

Printed in China

Contents

At the seaside

At the seaside,
there are lots
of things to do.

Paddling

You can paddle
in the sea.

Building a sand castle

It takes time to build a big sand castle.

9

Rock Pools

You can search the rock pools for sea creatures.

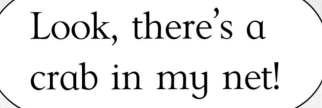

11

Beach games

It is fun to play with a bat and ball.

Picnics

You can eat a picnic on the beach.

15

Walking on the pier

You can walk along the pier.

Bouncy castl

You can jump on
the bouncy castle...

...or go down the
bouncy slide.

Merry-go-round!

The merry-go-round
will spin
you around.

Watching the sea

You can just sit and watch the sea.

Word bank

Look back for these words and pictures.

Bat and ball

Bouncy castle

Crab

Flag

Merry-go-round

Net

Paddling

Picnic

Pier

Rock pool

Sand castle

Sandwich